IT'S A CARIBOU!

by Kerry Dinmont

BUMBA BOOKS™

LERNER PUBLICATIONS ◆ MINNEAPOLIS

Note to Educators:

Throughout this book, you'll find critical thinking questions. These can be used to engage young readers in thinking critically about the topic and in using the text and photos to do so.

Lerner Publications Company
A division of Lerner Publishing Group, Inc.
241 First Avenue North
Minneapolis, MN 55401 USA

For reading levels and more information, look up this title at www.lernerbooks.com.

Library of Congress Cataloging–in–Publication Data

Names: Dinmont, Kerry, 1982– author.
Title: It's a caribou! / Kerry Dinmont.
Other titles: It is a caribou!
Description: Minneapolis : Lerner Publications, [2019] | Series: Bumba books. Polar animals | Audience: Ages 4–7. | Audience: K to grade 3. | Includes bibliographical references and index.
Identifiers: LCCN 2018000932 (print) | LCCN 2017057039 (ebook) | ISBN 9781512482843 (eb pdf) | ISBN 9781512482782 (lb : alk. paper) | ISBN 9781541526938 (pb : alk. paper)
Subjects: LCSH: Caribou—Juvenile literature.
Classification: LCC QL737.U55 (print) | LCC QL737.U55 D55 2019 (ebook) | DDC 599.65/8—dc23

LC record available at https://lccn.loc.gov/2018000932

Manufactured in the United States of America
1 – CG – 7/15/18

Table of
Contents

Caribou Travel 4

Parts of a Caribou 22

Picture Glossary 23

Read More 24

Index 24

Caribou Travel

Caribou are a kind of deer.

They live in polar areas.

Caribou are mammals.

Both males and females have antlers.

Why do you think caribou have antlers?

Thick fur keeps

caribou warm.

It is brown in summer and

lighter in winter.

Why do you think a caribou's fur changes color?

8

It is cold where caribou live.

They have fur on their noses.

It warms the air they breathe.

Caribou have hooves.

Hooves help caribou dig.

Hooves also help them swim.

Why might a caribou dig?

Caribou live in groups

called herds.

They travel to find food.

Caribou eat leaves

and plants.

They eat lichens too.

lichens

Mother caribou have one baby each year.

Baby caribou can stand soon after birth.

They travel with their mothers.

Caribou can run fast.

This helps them outrun predators.

Most caribou live about fifteen years.

Parts of a Caribou

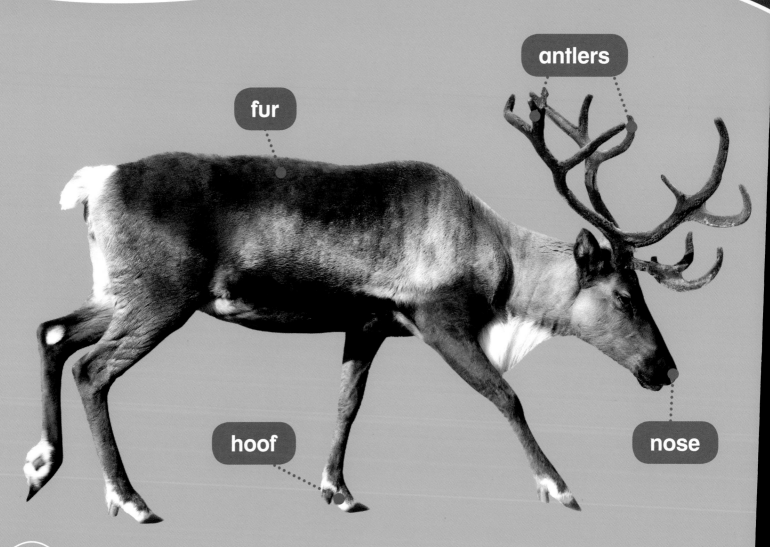

antlers

fur

hoof

nose

Picture Glossary

lichens

plantlike growths on rocks, walls, and trees

mammals

animals that give birth to live young and feed them milk

polar

a cold area near one of Earth's two poles

predators

animals that hunt other animals

Read More

Dinmont, Kerry. *It's a Polar Bear!* Minneapolis: Lerner Publications, 2019.

Meister, Cari. *Penguins*. Minneapolis: Jump!, 2014.

Owens, Mary Beth. *A Caribou Alphabet*. Thomaston, ME: Tilbury House, 2015.

Index

fur, 8, 11

herds, 15

hooves, 12

lichens, 16

mammals, 7

noses, 11

predators, 20

Photo Credits